D0903596

Tractors

by Mary Lindeen

BELLWETHER MEDIA • MINNEAPOLIS, MN

Note to Librarians, Teachers, and Parents:

Blastoff! Readers are carefully developed by literacy experts and combine standards-based content with developmentally appropriate text.

Level 1 provides the most support through repetition of high-frequency words, light text, predictable sentence patterns, and strong visual support.

Level 2 offers early readers a bit more challenge through varied simple sentences, increased text load, and less repetition of high-frequency words.

Level 3 advances early-fluent readers toward fluency through increased text and concept load, less reliance on visuals, longer sentences, and more literary language.

Whichever book is right for your reader, Blastoff! Readers are the perfect books to build confidence and encourage a love of reading that will last a lifetime!

This edition first published in 2007 by Bellwether Media.

Library of Congress Cataloging-in-Publication Data
Lindeen, Mary.
  Tractors / by Mary Lindeen.
     p. cm. – (Blastoff! Readers) (Mighty machines)
Summary: "Simple text and supportive full-color photographs introduce young readers to tractors. Intended for kindergarten through third grade"–Provided by publisher.
  Includes bibliographical references and index.
  ISBN-13: 978-1-60014-061-7 (hardcover : alk. paper)
  ISBN-10: 1-60014-061-0 (hardcover : alk. paper)
  1. Tractors–Pictorial works–Juvenile literature. I. Title.

  TL233.15.L55 2007
  629.225'2–dc22   2006035263

Contents

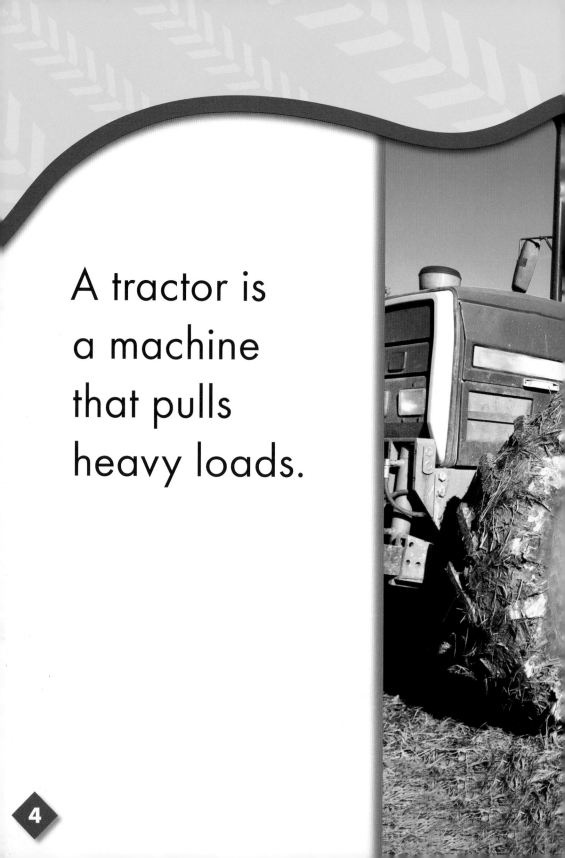

A tractor is
a machine
that pulls
heavy loads.

Most tractors
are used
on farms.

Tractors have
big tires.
They can go
through mud.

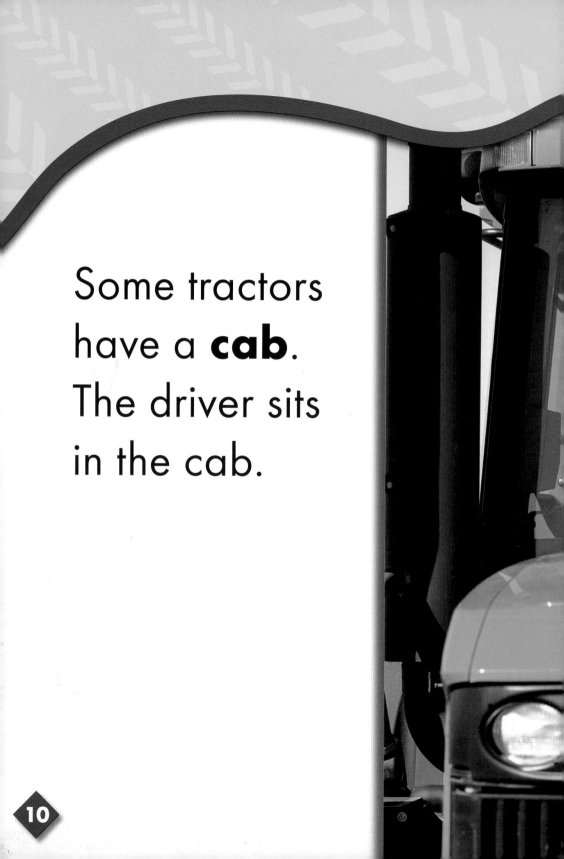

Some tractors have a **cab**. The driver sits in the cab.

A tractor has a **hitch**. A hitch hooks the tractor to machines that do many jobs.

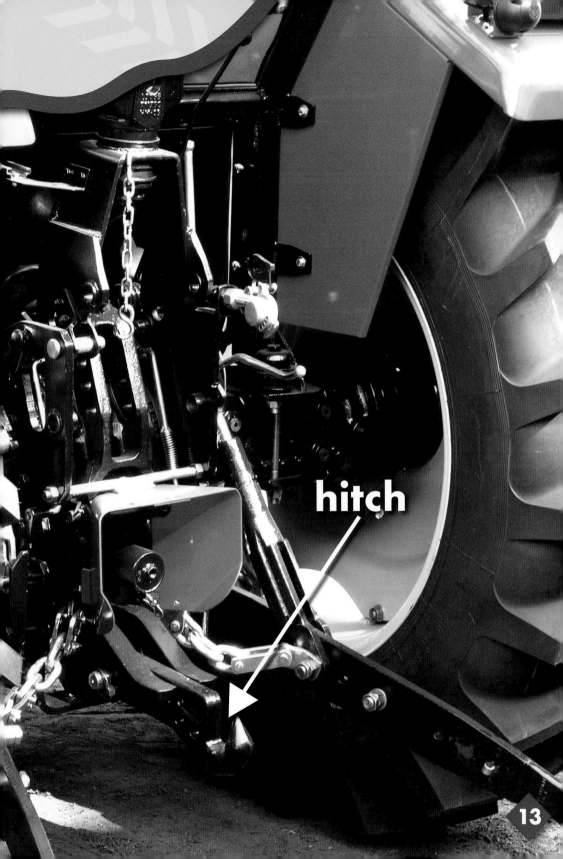

hitch

A tractor pulls a **plow**. A plow turns over the soil so farmers can plant seeds.

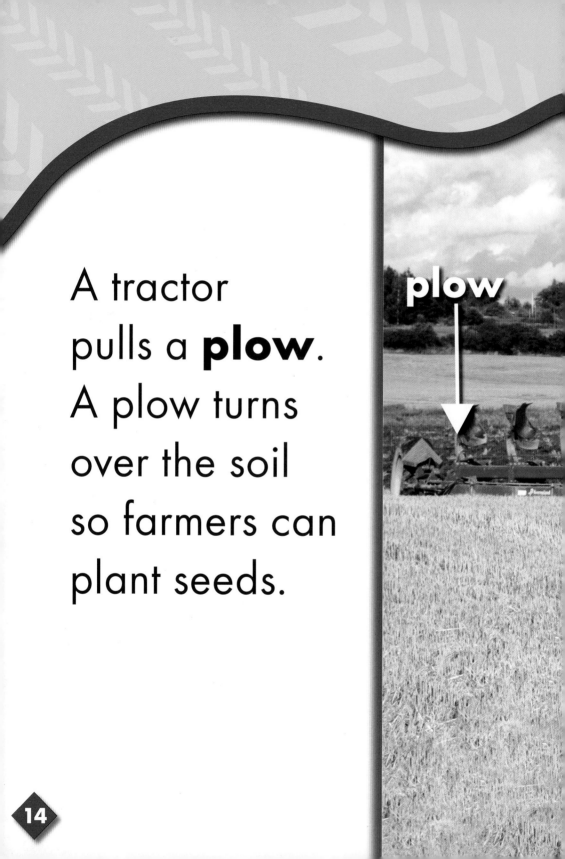

plow

A tractor pulls a **planter**. A planter puts seeds in the ground.

planter

A tractor pulls a **mower**. A mower cuts the grass.

mower

A tractor
starts a race.
Hang on!

Glossary

cab—a place for the driver to sit

hitch—the connection between a vehicle and a machine that the vehicle pulls behind it

mower—a machine that cuts down grass or plants

planter—a machine that plants seeds

plow—a machine that turns over soil to get it ready for planting

To Learn More

AT THE LIBRARY

Nelson, Kristin L. *Farm Tractors*. Minneapolis, Minn.: Lerner, 2002.

Tieck, Sarah. *Farm Tractors*. Edina, Minn.: ABDO, 2005.

Tractor. New York: DK Publishing, 2004.

ON THE WEB

Learning more about mighty machines is as easy as 1, 2, 3.

1. Go to www.factsurfer.com

2. Enter "mighty machines" into search box.

3. Click the "Surf" button and you will see a list of related web sites.

With factsurfer.com, finding more information is just a click away.

Index

The photographs in this book are reproduced through the courtesy of: Paul Prescott, front cover; Maurice van der Velden, p. 5; Chris Mellor/Getty Images, p. 7; texasmary, p. 9; Deere, Inc., pp. 11, 17, 19; Marek Pawluczuk, p. 13; Pixonet.com/Alamy, p. 15; Neil Phillip Mey, p. 21.